Improving the Curriculum: The Principal's Challenge

A Report of the NASSP Curriculum Council

DANIEL TANNER AND JAMES W. KEEFE, EDITORS

National Association of Secondary School Principals
1904 Association Drive, Reston, Virginia 22091

Scott D. Thomson, Executive Director, NASSP
Thomas F. Koerner, Director of Publications and Editorial Services
Carol Bruce, Associate Director of Publications
Eugenia Cooper Potter, Technical Editor

Copyright 1988
National Association of Secondary School Principals
1904 Association Drive
Reston, Virginia 22091
(703) 860-0200
ISBN 0-88210-215-X

Contents

Preface v

1. Toward a Contextually Grounded Curriculum 1
   Fenwick W. English

2. Practical Strategies for Improving the Curriculum 13
   Allan A. Glatthorn

3. Supervisory Leadership for Curriculum Renewal 19
   Daniel Tanner

4. Productive Time and Subject Matter Learning 26
   Herbert J. Walberg

NASSP Curriculum Advisory Council

Fenwick W. English
Professor and Chair
Educational Administration
College of Education
University of Cincinnati

Allan A. Glatthorn
School of Education
East Carolina University

Jane Stallings
Chair
Department of Curriculum and Instruction
College of Education
University of Houston

Daniel Tanner
Professor of Education
Graduate School of Education
Rutgers University

Herbert J. Walberg
College of Education
The University of Illinois at Chicago

James W. Keefe
Director of Research
NASSP

Preface

In May 1985, the NASSP Board of Directors approved the establishment of a Curriculum Council to assist the Association in developing and implementing a systematic agenda in curriculum and instruction. The Council was created to act as the research and development arm of NASSP's national Curriculum Committee.

From July 6 to 10, 1987, the Council conducted a National Curriculum Conference as an inservice program for interested members of the Association. The conference was held in Washington, D.C., and was attended by more than 60 educators from 28 states and territories and five foreign countries. The members of the Council would particularly like to recognize H. Jerome Freiberg of the University of Houston for his significant contribution to the conference, as well as issues subgroup reporters Tony Hanley, Claire W. Kondig, and Robert D. Winer, who organized and presented feedback from conference participants.

This publication, *Improving the Curriculum: The Principal's Challenge*, is an outgrowth of that conference. It is the second report of the Curriculum Council. The first report, *Rethinking Reform: The Principal's Dilemma*, was issued in late 1986.

Conference participants will recognize that the papers in this report are extensions of the presentations made in Washington, D.C. The reader will also note that the authors of the report express some divergent views, which serve to authenticate the "principal's challenge." Indeed, the intent of the Council was to engage the participants of the National Curriculum Conference in a forum for the open examination of problems, issues, and perspectives about the improvement of American secondary education.

Council members hope this report will provide a similar and stimulating forum for its readers.

D.T.
J.W.K.

CHAPTER 1

Toward a Contextually Grounded Curriculum

FENWICK W. ENGLISH

IN SCHOOL DISTRICT "X," the board of education reacts to a report documenting the fact that 63 percent of its high school graduates cannot name the seven continents by mandating this content for its social studies curriculum (Vitez, 1987). The high school principal calls the social studies department chair and teachers together to discuss the mandate. One teacher indicates he will not comply because he views the board's action as "precipitous" and "inappropriate." He believes that naming the seven continents is not important. It is more important that students understand the concept of "continental drift."

In school district "Y," the high school principal receives a memorandum from the commissioner of education notifying her that "global education" has been mandated by the state board of education as a graduation requirement in social studies beginning in September of the next school year. Faculty members inform the principal that they will file a grievance rather than eliminate electives to fit in global education. Several cite Secretary Bennett's negative reaction to global education as contained in the Rockefeller Foundation's recent report (Associated Press, 1987).

In school district "Z," a high school principal is asked to develop a magnet school for international relations. Students attending the school would study in various parts of the world. The principal recruits qualified faculty members to develop a curriculum for board approval.

These examples all raise the case for contextually grounded curriculum. The reality of formal curriculum development, however, is neither contextual nor very functional.

A perusal of many current curriculum texts would reveal a generic set of procedures to be used in all situations. These procedures are presented as "good," irrespective of the context. They are thought to be *context free*. Most seasoned school staff members would ignore such generalizations and tailor the procedures to the situation. They know that no decision is context free. All are *context bound*. One must know the situation before deciding what to do (Lincoln and Guba, 1985).

Situational knowledge is intimately connected with a firsthand understanding of the schooling context. This kind of understanding can lead to what Stake (1978) has called "tacit knowledge." Tacit knowledge is acquired by doing something in the real world. When human beings interact and learn, they make modifications, often unconsciously. As they continue to do this over time they acquire a fundamental understanding of things very different from the theoretical or purely conceptual.

Many curriculum texts with context-free generalizations have been written by authors who have never been principals or who have no direct administrative experience in schools. They lack the "tacit knowledge" base so essential to knowing what will work administratively and what will not.

A school is a special kind of social entity. It is a contrived reality with a special context for those who work there (English, 1987). A school is understood by an experienced principal in a very different way than by someone who has not been a school administrator.

Contextually grounded curriculum development begins with an intellectual and tacit understanding about schools as workplaces (Dreeben, 1973). A school is a particular kind of work organization in our society. It is a formal organization because it represents a specific set of repetitive societal activities. The unique combination of a school's physical, spatial, interpersonal, and task-related realities results in a form or structure. The school principal is concerned with the creation and control of that structure. It is *the* fundamental task of management (Tausky, 1970).

Understanding the relationship between curriculum and control in schools is the key to unlocking their potential for effectiveness. Indeed, effectiveness itself can only be judged by understanding the specific context that produces any curriculum.

Contextually grounded curriculum has a kind of "goodness of fit" in which professional practice is shaped by, and in turn shapes, the social environment. No practice, or assumption from which practice emanates, should be assumed to be correct until a kind of environmental sensing validates the *reality* of the situation. Curriculum development must "fit" the context. In this sense, curriculum development must be "grounded" first in context and then defined and applied. There are no universal curricular practices that are good for all times and all places. There are no context-free principles that are immune to the influences of a specific time and situation.

Current proposals for "teacher empowerment" that propose to free teachers from organizational constraints would be viewed as irresponsible romanticism in school districts like our hypothetical "X" and "Y." No school can ignore or defy a policy-legal mandate and not find itself at risk. Bottom-up curriculum development works only in contexts like hypothetical district "Z."

Forces Shaping Curricula in Schools

Curriculum has been subservient to organization and method (control) almost since the inception of schooling in North America.

Early educational texts rarely, if ever, mentioned curriculum. For example, a mid-nineteenth century text called *The School and the Schoolmaster* (Potter and Emerson, 1842) never uses the word curriculum in its 538 pages. Much time is spent on instruction, school organization, moral education, and the training of teachers. Sections are devoted to such school subjects as reading, spelling, grammar, writing, drawing, arithmetic, accounts, geography, history, physiology, composition, and government. Attention is paid to the size, location, layout, lighting, heating, and ventilation of the school house. But there is nothing about the curriculum.

The role of the curriculum as the basis for continuity in a school was not examined until schools became more complex (i.e., graded). In 1842, the requirements for a system only extended to a one room school house in rural areas and slightly less primitive structures in the cities. The authors of *The School and the Schoolmaster* placed responsibility squarely on the teacher, since few principals existed at that time:

> The teacher is to establish a system of organization, the object of which is to prevent irregularities, and to save time; to enable him to do as much for each, and for all, as possible; and to exercise each pupil according to his capacity and advancement, not overtasking him, nor leaving him unoccupied. This system should be comprehensive enough to embrace all operations of the school, and so simple that all the children may be able to understand it; so that, when once established, it shall almost keep itself in operation, leaving the teacher his whole time for other duties. (p. 394)

Five years after the publication of the Potter and Emerson text, the graded school emerged as the organizational form designed to cope with mushrooming enrollments and the need for control, both of students and costs. Evidence of graded organization is supplied by the 1866 *Report of the Superintendent of Common Schools of the Commonwealth of Pennsylvania*.

The Superintendent commented:

> . . .an ungraded school is an imperfect school. Wherever a sufficient number of pupils can be brought together, it is very much better and cheaper to grade the schools—better, because it provides a way in which the higher branches can be taught, and it renders classification more easy and teaching more effective; and cheaper, because with the same number of pupils it does not require the same teaching force. (Wickersham, p. ix.)

The Superintendent issued a call to "carry on the work of grading rapidly. It is our next step in advance." At this time only 15 percent of Pennsylvania's 13,146 schools were graded.

Some 20 years later, Pennsylvania State Superintendent E. E. Higbee sensed that gradedness was a mixed blessing indeed:

> This rapid increase of graded schools demands most careful watchfulness upon the part of superintendents and teachers. While we have great gain derived from such division of labor as the graded school secures, we must seek to avoid the serious dangers involved. Teachers, confined to one line of studies, and those that are suited only to a certain age, are apt to take into view only the small section of a child's life belonging to that age, and this weakens the great incentive to work which comes from the clear vision of the end of education in the beginning .... great caution is required for graded schools, lest, through anxiety to promote from grade to grade, the child be fitted more for examination than for life. (Higbee, 1889, pp. iii-iv.)

The issue underlying gradedness is that of control reached by a specialization of labor. Administrative control is surely gained, but at the same time, teachers lose personal and holistic control of the educational process. In 1842, it was realistic to expect a teacher to establish a system of organization for the entire school because the teacher did all the work.

By 1889, it was no longer possible. Now the content of teaching was captured in smaller pieces by courses of study. The control of the totality of the school was lost to the teacher by division and separation of labor. (See Apple, 1979.)

It was no coincidence that *curriculum as a concept* arose only after gradedness was almost completely established. The first professional book about curriculum was not printed until almost 1900 (Schubert, 1980). It was also no accident that the early proponents of a standardized curriculum were superintendents of schools in the nation's largest cities. Administrative control and curricular hegemony were, almost from the beginning, two sides of the same coin (Tyack, 1974). Current state competency testing and reforms are simply extensions of the same logic.

These historical traces vividly illustrate that the overwhelming contextual impetus for curriculum development in schools was rooted in control. They also show that, as school systems grew, guidelines and departmentalization solved one problem and created another. From both a school and a district perspective, administrators and teachers must confront the problems of instructional coordination within grades and articulation across grades and buildings. Ways must be found of bridging across the individual units to create a focus among them. The curriculum remains the most potent and tangible vehicle to do just that.

Curriculum Management in Secondary Schools

Curriculum management is the application of curricular ideas in operational settings, most often in schools. Because the growth of curriculum historically has been intimately connected to the establishment and extension of administrative control in schools, many of its guiding ideas are from organizational theory (Hall, 1972) and design (Galbraith, 1977), not from philosophy or psychology.

Curriculum management is a kind of hybrid field, something like biochemistry, in which the models, modes, and procedures of two fields are merged into a new one (English, 1986-87a). One result of this hybrid origin is that curriculum can be viewed as the work plan for a school. As such, it ought to be purposive, connected to goals and policies, and translated into what people ought to do in schools; i.e., real work.

Curriculum is contextually defined by its control system and setting, and is concerned about moving from plans to operations, from design to delivery. It is shaped by some powerful ideas about work design. One of these ideas is the concept of quality control (Juran, 1974). Quality control has been defined as establishing "fitness for use."

Its application in the field of curriculum management is shown in Figure 1. Here, fitness for use means that the work plan is responsive to

Figure 1
Quality Control in Schools*

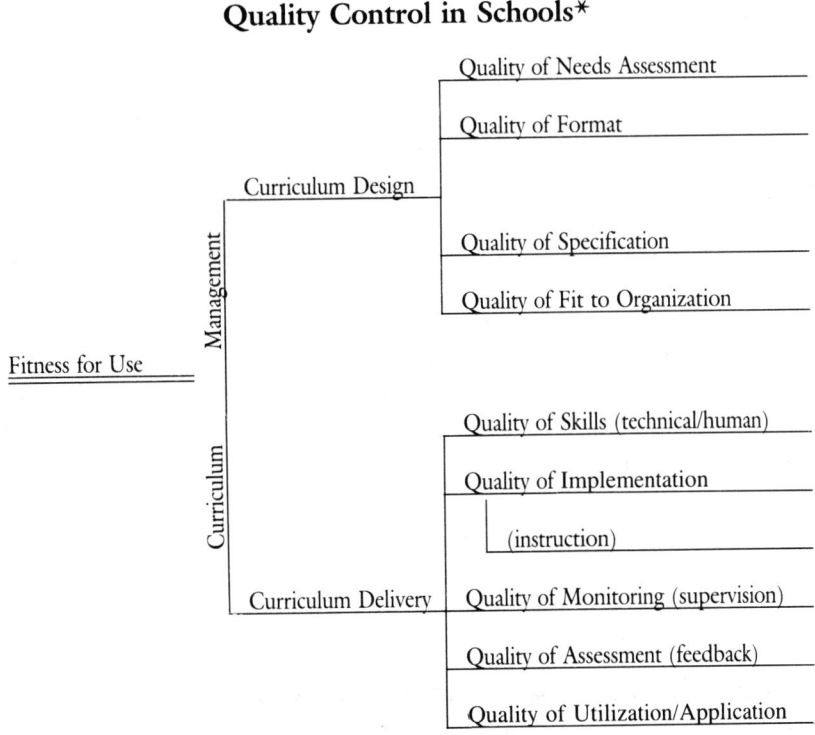

* *From F.W. English,* Curriculum Management *(1987) Charles C. Thomas, Publisher. Used with permission.*

its environment and enables those who use it to accomplish their purposes.

One can see immediately that, depending upon point of view and motivation, curriculum may be "fit for use" by one group and unfit for another. Administrators, for example, may want the curriculum to provide an overall focus for teaching across many grade levels. If the curriculum offers this focus, administrators are satisfied because administration's job is direction and control (Drucker, 1974).

If a teacher wants to do something innovative or idiosyncratic, however, a fixed curriculum that intrudes on this personal agenda may be viewed as unsatisfactory. Much of the conflict about curriculum, its content and specification, is about the authority to define and deliver what someone has determined to be most appropriate, exclusive of anyone else. Curriculum per se is not the issue. Autonomy is the real issue (Lortie, 1975).

Current calls for "trusting teachers" miss the mark. The issue is not one of trust. The issue is one of work design, contextually grounded. If a school is functioning within an environment of "high stakes testing," (Popham, 1987) and the consequences of not being responsive are severe, the work plan must be specific and tight. The plan must link instruction to measurement through curriculum alignment. The higher student and staff mobility factors are, the more the work plan must compensate for these negative variables. The higher the level of skills to be assessed, the less likely pupils will learn them outside school and the more likely learning must depend on a highly sequenced and structured curriculum.

When work tasks are complex and require a high level of coordination, can any individual have much latitude to change a plan developed by a designated and authorized group? Some modifications will always be required to respond to learner needs. This kind of flexibility demands some built-in autonomy for teacher decision making. A lock-step curriculum, mechanically delivered, works against a school being responsive in a high stakes testing environment.

But unless it can be shown that learners have already mastered the designated curriculum content, teachers should not have the autonomy to ignore what is included in the curriculum. No curriculum can be designed without knowing the context in which the curriculum and the teacher are to function. Context is always specific to a situation. Contextually grounded curriculum begins with a situational analysis, and then proceeds to a responsive work plan.

Figure 1 lists nine elements of quality control within the framework of curriculum management. Four deal with curriculum design and five with curriculum delivery. We will briefly discuss the criteria for quality control in the sections that follow.

Curriculum Design Criteria

Quality of Needs Assessment

Needs assessment is the process that determines what objectives the curriculum will embrace. It is very much a value laden process. Educators are always guided by certain assumptions in selecting the outcomes of schooling. In some cases, the process goes on without individuals even being conscious of the values involved (Apple, 1980). Needs assessment identifies specific "gaps" between actual student performance and desired or required student performance. Curriculum is then designed to close the gaps or "meet the needs." (Kaufman and English, 1979.)

If a school is located in an environment that supports wide variations in pupil accomplishment, that fosters a diversified program within a differentiated curriculum, and that applies assessment/accountability broadly, then needs assessment can be very broad. The work plan, in turn, may be very open-ended, which permits and encourages teacher initiatives and responses.

On the other hand, if a school is functioning within an environment of accountability, the needs assessment must focus on the required outcomes and identify where student performance is lacking. The result may be a very detailed, specific, and narrow plan that must be followed very closely.

Quality of Format

Most curriculum guides produced by school systems are notoriously dysfunctional (English, 1986-87b). The guides are not constructed to be functional. They are bulky and very difficult to use, and rarely assist teachers in making useful content-inclusion decisions. Very few contain information about alignment to texts or testing. Most are collections of methods or activities which experienced teachers find unnecessary or even counterproductive (Eisner, 1967).

Curriculum guides should fit the work context. They should provide the "connectedness" required within a school and a school system to be responsive to its environment. Loose or open-ended work statements only fit work situations where outcomes are not considered important, or where standardized testing is not employed.

Quality of Specification

Specificity is determined by the nature of the work and the outcomes desired. If outcomes are complex, highly cumulative, and dependent upon time to learn, a high level of specificity about the work itself will be necessary. The work plan must include the required content, pacing, and sequencing information, as well as the assessment practices that will evaluate learning.

Specificity can never be context free. For example, behavioral objectives have been misused in curriculum guides as agents of specificity. These objectives are not statements about the work to be performed; they are statements of the ways the work, once done, will be assessed. When assessment is substituted for a work statement, the work (curriculum) may be corrupted by inadequate assessment. The work ought not to be shaped, *a priori,* by the measurement process. Measurement should follow design. Curriculum development/design, as it is being created, must be free from the yoke of measurement.

Quality of Fit to the Organization

The school curriculum is normally designed to be congruent with the work organization in which it will operate. Most principals inherit an existing school. The school incorporates a structure and procedures that enable it to function more or less well on a day-to-day basis. The curriculum represents one aspect of the context of schooling; the school schedule another.

Curriculum that is predicated on false assumptions is often reshaped to the school by scheduling ingenuity. Some powerful curriculum ideas have been stunted, once scheduled (Glatthorn, 1986).

The purpose of schooling is to organize learning. Schools are organizations. To exist they must be managed. School organization should not be considered a "natural state." It is neither "natural" nor necessarily the best in its current form. It is easy to argue about curriculum apart from any sustained analysis of the context into which the curriculum is to be placed. Curriculum management asks for what ends and for which purposes?

No curriculum should be blindly fitted to any organization. Indeed, principals themselves are the products of schooling. They must also become students of the processes by which their own thinking has been shaped. They must learn to analyze their own curriculum biases before deciding to perpetuate them.

Curriculum Delivery Criteria

Quality of Skills

A sophisticated curriculum must be placed in equally sophisticated hands to be delivered as designed. Teachers are the primary agents for curriculum delivery. It is necessary to assess the existing range of skills among the teaching staff to know if the curriculum can be delivered appropriately.

Sometimes districts create problems for teachers. It is one thing to design a curriculum that requires changes of emphasis within the range of teaching behaviors. It is another to cement those changes to new technology. Teachers must learn how to use new technology before they can apply a new curriculum. Improperly trained teachers place curriculum reform in a kind of double jeopardy.

Quality of Implementation

Contextually grounded curriculum is also dependent on teacher understanding of a rapport with students, their interests, motivations, problems, and skills. The classroom is the typical context for working out these issues of curriculum delivery.

The ways of implementing a curriculum within a classroom appear to be almost limitless. No curriculum developer can anticipate every situation that might confront teachers, so there will always be a need for teacher ingenuity. Yet, the context also limits the choices. Schools facing external demands for improvement must proceed in a different manner than those not facing these constraints.

Administrators and teachers, working with a specific curriculum, can create closer linkages between the written, taught, and tested curricula and improve pupil performance as a result (Niedermeyer and Yelon, 1981). Instead of arguing about what kind of situation appears to be best irrespective of the situation at hand, contextually grounded curriculum accepts the fact that different outcomes demand different means to elicit them. The propriety of instructional approach within any curriculum must be defined by the context, and not in the abstract.

Quality of Monitoring

Monitoring is checking to see that the curriculum has been implemented as designed. Most principals use two major procedures to monitor the delivery of curriculum: observation, and reviewing lesson plan books. Neither one is very effective as conventionally practiced.

Imagine a typical secondary school curriculum offering more than 300 courses. School administrators are confronted with an enormous initial problem in simply understanding the entire curriculum. Most administrators are not subject matter specialists, but generalists. Observation may be effective in assessing the generic characteristics of effective teaching behavior, but it typically does not involve any detailed inquiry of curricular propriety, pacing, or sequencing.

A review of plan books suffers from the same shortcomings. Typically, what appears as content in most plan books is not referenced to a specific curriculum. Without that linkage, the extent to which the plan book actually covers the curriculum is unknown.

The fact is that principals rarely monitor the curriculum. They monitor teaching. Teaching may or may not be guided by a curriculum. Much of what has been defined as the curriculum of a school may not actually influence teaching in a given classroom.

The first step for a principal is not to monitor the curriculum, but to ensure that the curriculum is known and utilized by teachers as they shape daily and weekly lessons. Then, when administrators review plans or observe a class, the teaching will represent the curriculum.

Quality of Assessment (Feedback)

Feedback is important for at least two reasons. First, feedback may indicate how much teaching has achieved the learning objectives embodied in the curriculum. Second, feedback tells teachers and administrators what has actually happened in the classroom. Some organizational thinkers believe that organizations, even with formal plans, act first and think later. They are not directed so much by rational models of planning as by analysis of past actions to discover what they were trying to do at a given time (Weick, 1985).

A good deal of teaching is like that. There are occasions when a teacher looks back over the plan book to get a sense of what was happening in a particular lesson. Creative teaching is always somewhat spontaneous. To capture a sense of the moment, a lesson plan may be abandoned. In such cases, lesson plans are really rationalizations for what the teacher was trying to do instead of a template for teaching.

In either case, feedback is useful. Connections must be established between the feedback, the curriculum, and the actions of the teacher. Often the curriculum is so nebulous that it is impossible to use feedback to check whether the curriculum was delivered properly.

In some instances, even test data are reported at different levels than required by curriculum guides. This incongruity may make it almost impossible to link the information on pupil growth to the larger curriculum. Feedback must be understood to be applied.

Quality of Utilization/Application

The quality of utilization and further application is dependent on the congruence between what was attempted and some predetermined plan or guide. With a work record, data on performance can be evaluated because it can be related to the actual work performed.

A curriculum work plan must exist that fosters coordinated action; the will must be present to apply the plan, and to use feedback to improve performance over time. Curriculum is the work plan that connects all the pieces and parts of a school and a school system. The curriculum provides focus for thousands of tasks and organizes them into meaningful activity characterized by consistency, continuity, and flexibility.

Summary

No school is exactly like any other school. The context of each school is unique. Whatever the environment, curriculum should enable a school to be more effective. The environmental constraints and the patterns of action and reaction in a school are sufficiently varied to require that the development of its curriculum reflect contextual forces rather than some generalized model or set of guidelines. Curriculum, to be functional, must be relational and transactional. It must be contextually grounded.

References

Apple, M.W. *Ideology and Curriculum*. Boston: Routledge and Kegan Paul, 1979.

_____. "Analyzing Determinations: Understanding and Evaluating the Production of Social Outcomes in Schools." *Curriculum Inquiry*, Spring 1980, pp. 55-76.

Associated Press. "Students Faulted on Global Issues." *New York Times*. May 13, 1987, p. B 10.

Dreeben, R. "The School as a Workplace." In *Second Handbook of Research on Teaching*, edited by R.M.W. Travers. Chicago, Ill.: Rand McNally, 1973.

Drucker, P.F. *Management*. New York: Harper & Row, 1974.

Eisner, E.W. "Educational Objectives: Help or Hindrance?" *School Review*, Autumn 1967, pp. 250-60.

English, F.W. "Educational Administration and Curriculum Management." *National Forum of Educational Administration and Supervision Journal* 4 (1986-87a):22-23.

_____. "It's Time To Abolish Conventional Curriculum Guides." *Educational Leadership*, December 1986/January 1987b, pp. 50-53.

_____. *Curriculum Management*. Springfield, Ill.: Charles C. Thomas Publisher, 1987.

Galbraith, J.R. *Organization Design*. Reading, Mass.: Addison-Wesley Publishing Co., 1977.

Glatthorn, A.A. "How Does the School Schedule Affect the Curriculum?" *Rethinking Reform: The Principal's Dilemma*, edited by H.J. Walberg and J.W. Keefe. Reston, Va.: National Association of Secondary School Principals, 1986.

Hall, R.H. *Organizations*. Englewood Cliffs, N.J.: Prentice-Hall, 1972.

Higbee, E.E. *Report of the Superintendent of Public Instruction of the Commonwealth of Pennsylvania*. Harrisburg, Pa.: Edwin K. Meyers, State Printer, 1889.

Juran, J.M. "Basic Concepts." In *Quality Control Handbook*. New York: McGraw-Hill, 1974.

Kaufman, R.A., and English, F.W. *Needs Assessment*. Englewood Cliffs, N.J.: Educational Technology Publications, 1979.

Lincoln, Y.S., and Guba, E.G. *Naturalistic Inquiry.* Beverly Hills, Calif.: SAGE Publications, 1985.

Lortie, D.C. *Schoolteacher.* Chicago, Ill.: University of Chicago Press, 1975.

Niedermeyer, F., and Yelon, S. "Los Angeles Aligns Instruction with Essential Skills." *Educational Leadership,* May 1981, pp. 618-20.

Popham, W.J. "The Merits of Measurement-Driven Instruction." *Phi Delta Kappan,* May 1987, pp. 687-88.

Potter, A., and Emerson, G.B. *The School and the Schoolmaster.* New York: Harper and Brothers, 1842.

Schubert, W.H. *Curriculum Books.* Washington, D.C.: University Press of America, 1980.

Spring, J. *The American School 1642-1985.* New York: Longman, 1986.

Stake, R.E. "The Case Study Method in Social Inquiry." *Educational Researcher* 7 (1978):5-8.

Tausky, C. *Work Organizations.* Itasca, Ill.: F.E. Peacock Publishers, 1970.

Tyack, D.B. *The One Best System.* Cambridge: Harvard University Press, 1974.

Vitez, M. "It's 1987: Do You Know Where Your Country Is?" *The Philadelphia Inquirer,* June 10, 1987, p. D 1.

Weick, K. "Sources of Order in Underorganized Systems: Themes in Recent Organizational Theory." In *Organizational Theory and Inquiry: The Paradigm Revolution,* edited by Y.S. Lincoln. Beverly Hills, Calif.: SAGE Publications, 1985.

Wickersham, J.P. *Report of the Superintendent of Common Schools of the Commonwealth of Pennsylvania.* Harrisburg, Pa.: Singerly and Myers, State Printers, 1867.

Chapter 2

Practical Strategies for Improving The Curriculum

Allan A. Glatthorn

Periodically, Principals Are asked to exercise leadership in implementing a comprehensive program of curriculum revision. It is more important to the daily operation of the school, however, that principals also know the strategies of what might be called curricular incrementalism—or, more simply, tinkering with the curriculum.

A strategy of incremental change consumes much less time, money, and effort, and properly managed can, in time, make a significant difference. In this chapter, I would like to suggest six practical strategies for bringing about incremental improvement.

1. *Add a course in applied problem solving.*

One of the interesting aspects of the current movement to teach critical thinking is how academic it all seems. Most of the programs seem to focus unduly on using critical thinking in the classroom, teaching such skills as identifying cause and effect in the social studies, analyzing the meaning of a literary work, solving mathematical problems, and analyzing data in the science laboratory. Obviously, these subject-related skills are important, for school is central in the lives of the young.

But, there seems to be an even greater need to teach what might be termed applied problem solving—the application of critical thinking skills in real-life situations. An applied problem-solving course might meet three times a week (paired perhaps with study skills), include a heterogeneous group of students, and be taught by a team of teachers with varied academic and experimental backgrounds. It would emphasize decision making and problem solving about the important issues that confront young people. The focus would be on the process, helping students learn how to integrate rationality and intuition in making wise choices.

One possible formulation of such a course is presented in Figure 1, although it makes more sense for it to be designed by teachers themselves who can tailor it to a given group of students.

2. *Reduce curriculum coverage and add curriculum depth.*

Principals should know how to reduce the curriculum. I believe that one of our critical problems in education is curricular obesity—a swollen curriculum that tries to cover too much territory.

Figure 1
Content Outline: Applied Problem Solving

1. An overview of problem-solving approaches.
2. The next five years: making career and educational choices.
3. Making major consumer purchases.
4. Making moral choices: value-based problem solving.
5. The computer in problem solving: uses and limitations.
6. Solving environmental problems: balancing complex demands.
7. Using the media intelligently.
8. Problem solving at election time: thinking critically about politics.
9. Zen and the art of not solving problems: problem solving in non-western cultures.

Consider what happens in most language arts curricula when teachers teach grammar. The fifth grade teacher conscientiously tries to teach all the parts of speech and all the parts of the sentence. The students retain about 10 percent of what they have studied.

The following year, the sixth grade teacher asks with a scowl, "Who was your fifth grade teacher?" and races through the same content—with the same results. Then the seventh grade teacher asks with a frown, "Where did you go to school last year?" So it goes, year after year, teaching too much, with very little mastery.

In many subjects, schools would be wise to teach less better: to reduce coverage for the sake of depth. The key is to find a team of willing teachers and to ask them to shrink the content by about one-third, ruthlessly eliminating all except the essentials. (See NASSP Task Force, 1982, for a general model.)

Consider what might be done with the time saved in, for example, the field of social studies:

- Students might undertake their own primary research, making the community a laboratory.
- The teacher might provide remedial instruction for students who do not achieve mastery and offer enrichment for those who do.
- The teacher might add depth to several of the units, bringing in primary source material and teaching students how to evaluate sources.
- In one or two units, teachers might use an interdisciplinary approach, examining, for instance, how the war in Vietnam affected both the arts and the sciences.

3. *Add a course or unit in creativity.*

Educators have always given a great deal of lip service to the goal of making students more creative—but have never done much about it. It may be time to make a frontal attack on the problem by teaching for creativity. This kind of course or unit would be a laboratory, one that would have students thinking and working creatively, not just talking about creativity.

Figure 2 shows an outline for such an interdisciplinary course, although, again, it might well be developed by those who teach it.

Figure 2
Content Outline: Creativity

1. The creative spirit: an historical perspective.
2. Creating with words: writing poetry and stories.
3. The nature of visual creativity: drawing from the right brain.
4. Creative problem solving: combining creativity and critical thinking.
5. Creating with materials: fabric, wood, plastic, metals.
6. Creativity in the home: the design of environments for living.
7. The computer and creativity: possibilities and limitations.
8. Fostering personal creativity.
9. The limits of creativity and the uses of conformity.

Observe one major advantage to this approach. It brings together teachers who do not often communicate and asks them to share ideas from their unique perspectives. English, art, music, home economics, science, and industrial arts each include elements of creative thinking and production. The laboratory might help students understand, for example, that creating with fabric or with wood is just as important as creating with words.

4. *Re-institute selected elective courses.*

This suggestion obviously amounts to heresy at a time when almost all the experts are talking about rigor, standardization, and uniformity. I believe, however, that we gave up too easily on elective courses. They were never subjected to rigorous evaluation.

The experts who blamed these courses for a decline in SAT scores did so on the basis of scant evidence. Clearly, many ill-designed elective courses existed, assembled by busy teachers who simply taught what they felt like teaching. But it is possible to design electives in ways that also teach essential skills. (See Glatthorn, 1980, for one process to use with English electives.)

Carefully-designed elective programs should be offered from grades 6 through 10. The pressures of college entrance and the expectations of parents and employers probably make required offerings necessary for high school juniors and seniors. But educators can broaden student experience in the lower grades, and they should avail themselves of that opportunity.

The advantages of well-designed elective programs are several. They resolve the arguments over ability grouping by bringing students together on the basis of interest. They enable teachers to teach in their areas of expertise. And they provide a leavening effect in what might otherwise be a very heavy and dull curriculum.

5. *Develop experiential curricula for marginal students.*

Clear evidence exists that many of the curriculum reforms urged on us by the national reform commissions can penalize marginal students. (See ASCD, 1985, for an excellent summary of the evidence here.)

Tenacious observers like John Goodlad (1984) have documented the banality and boredom of the curriculum for the less able. Obviously, something must be done.

What will be most effective for these students? One of the most promising means of improving the achievement and facilitating the development of at-risk youth is the use of field experiences for experiential learning. Wehlage (1983) believes that carefully structured field experiences would help marginal students achieve what he calls social bonding, a developmental process for forming commitment to and involvement in the life of home and school.

There are two prerequisites for such bonding to take place: adolescents must develop the ability to use abstract thinking and they must shift from an egocentric to a sociocentric point of view.

Wehlage's research has led him to conclude that effective experiential programs embody five principles:

- First, they provide optimal challenge with manageable conflict.
- Second, they require students to take initiative and responsibility.
- Third, the program experiences are perceived by young people to have integrity and dignity.
- Fourth, they provide youth with opportunities for acquiring a sense of competence and success.
- Fifth, systematic opportunities are available for the participants to reflect about their experiences.

Many such programs are already being implemented. We simply must offer them for all marginal adolescents, not just those fortunate enough to be in schools that have undertaken early leadership.

6. *Try the "cooperative mastery" model.*

The cooperative mastery model (Glatthorn, 1987) attempts to combine the advantages of direct instruction and cooperative learning. As Rosenshine and Stevens (1986) have pointed out, direct instruction is especially useful when teaching younger students, slower students, and students of all ages and abilities during the first stages of instruction on unfamiliar material. Too many supervisors and teachers, however, rely too much on the direct instruction model and ignore the well-supported advantages of cooperative learning.

In their review of the research, two of its principal proponents, Johnson and Johnson (1985) reach this conclusion: Cooperative learning experiences, when compared with competitive and individual ones, result in higher achievement, promote greater competencies in critical thinking, develop more positive attitudes toward the subject, and lead students to believe that the grading system is fair.

The cooperative mastery model works this way:

- A team of teachers and supervisors analyze and classify the existing curriculum in a particular subject into three categories: the mastery curriculum, those essential concepts and skills that can best be taught with a whole-class, direct instruction approach; the cooperative curriculum, those essential concepts and skills that can best be taught through cooperative learning; and the enrichment curriculum, units that students can learn on their own.
- The teacher teaches each mastery unit with direct instruction. Students take a mastery test at the conclusion of the unit. Those achieving less than 90 percent spend additional time on remedial work, getting help from computers and student tutors.
- Students not giving or receiving remediation work independently on enrichment units.
- When the remediation and independent study have been concluded, all students work together in cooperative learning groups on the content identified for the cooperative curriculum. In most instances, cooperative groups would work on laboratory and inquiry projects, applying what they have learned in the mastery units and extending their knowledge.

The chief advantage of the cooperative mastery model is that it attempts to match research-based instruction to the components of the curriculum where it may work the best. Rather than use direct instruction, or mastery learning, or cooperative learning with the entire curriculum, cooperative mastery attempts to create an optimal match.

These are the six incremental changes that any principal can make. They will not transform schools, but they should make the curriculum a bit more exciting and productive for all students.

References

ASCD Task Force on Increased High School Graduation Requirements. *With Consequences for All.* Alexandria, Va.: Association for Supervision and Curriculum Development, 1985.

Glatthorn, A.A. *A Guide for Developing an English Curriculum for the Eighties.* Urbana, Ill.: National Council of Teachers of English, 1980.

——————. *Curriculum Renewal.* Alexandria, Va.: Association for Supervision and Curriculum Development, 1987.

Goodlad, J.I. *A Place Called School: Prospects for the Future.* New York: McGraw-Hill, 1984.

Johnson, D.W., and Johnson, R.R. "Cooperative Learning and Adaptive Instruction." In *Adapting Instruction to Individual Differences,* edited by M.C. Wang and H.J. Walberg. Berkeley, Calif.: McCutchan, 1985.

NASSP Task Force. *Reducing the Curriculum: A Process Model.* Reston, Va.: NASSP, 1982.

Rosenshine, B., and Stevens, R. "Teaching Functions." In *Handbook of Research on Teaching* (3rd ed.), edited by M.D. Wittrock. New York: Macmillan, 1986.

Wehlage, G.G. "The Marginal High School Student: Defining the Problem and Searching for Policy." *Children and Youth Services Review* 5 (1983):321-42.

Chapter 3

Supervisory Leadership For Curriculum Renewal

Daniel Tanner

Before the Turn of the century, the dominant mode of educational supervision was inspection. Lay committees from local school boards, often unschooled themselves, joined the school administrator to examine prospective teachers for certification and to inspect teachers' classrooms for deficiencies.

During the early decades of this century, a pronounced shift occurred from inspectional supervision to production supervision as school administrators cast themselves in the production-efficiency mode of the industrial or business manager. Standards were set for students as educational products, and the efficiency of the enterprise of schooling was to be assessed by the ratio of output measures over inputs or cost factors (Callahan, 1962).

This may sound familiar. The production model of supervision has been revived during various periods of perceived educational crisis since midcentury.

Recognition must also be given to the struggle on the part of experimentalist-progressive educators throughout the first half of the twentieth century to develop an entirely new mode of school supervision, a democratic-participatory approach based on the Deweyan concept of problem solving for educational improvement. This mode of supervision engaged administrators, supervisors, and teachers in the cooperative formulation, implementation, and evaluation of educational policy and in curriculum development.

A leading proponent and practitioner of this mode of supervision was Jesse Newlon, who, as superintendent of schools, instituted it in the Denver schools in 1922. According to Lawrence Cremin (1971), Newlon's program was "probably the first in which classroom teachers participated significantly in a system-wide effort at reform."

Within a few years, Newlon's program in Denver gained national recognition to the point that the literature in school administration increasingly recognized supervision and curriculum development as an interrelated process. As Clement put the matter in 1927, "In the instance of administrative practice, supervision of instruction and curriculum development should operate conjointly."

The theoretical foundation for a unified approach to curriculum and instruction was developed by Dewey who, as early as 1899, pointed out that the separation of subject matter and method "is a survival of the medieval philosophical dualism." Such a separation is like having the learner engage in the act of reading apart from the material through which the act derives meaning. Reading material does not attain working power until it is transformed into meaning in the life of the learner.

Yet, despite the efforts of experimentalist-progressive educators, and the burgeoning body of research supporting the democratic-participatory/ problem-solving mode of supervision, production supervision remained the dominant practice through the early decades of the twentieth century.

Hollis Caswell (1942) spoke out repeatedly on the need to transform the structure and practice of supervision. He reiterated a call for democratic-participatory supervision: "Participation of all members of the school staff should be recognized as essential to the formulation of educational policies, and the individual school should be made the operational unit in program development."

The Swedish social economist, Gunnar Myrdal (1962), observed that ". . . teachers in America have not even been allowed to have as much power over the government of their own schools as they have in comparable (European) countries. Their status as employees is stressed."

Production Supervision—A Dysfunctional Approach

Today, we find a renewed trend toward the identification of curriculum with educational policy above and beyond the purview of the supervisor and teacher. The narrow charge to the supervisor and teacher is instructional delivery and instructional improvement.

How can we account for this renewed trend toward segmentation and isolation when the professionalism of our work requires a sense of unity and shared responsibility in policy and practice, in curriculum development and instruction? I see two chief forces accounting for this segmentation in our professional activity.

First, during periods of perceived national crisis, there is the tendency to construe curriculum reform as a policy matter beyond the scope of those in the school and classroom. The work of the supervisor becomes merely technical—implementing policy established at a higher level of authority within, or even external to, the educational system in which the supervisor and teacher work. In effect, the professionalism of the supervisor and teacher is diminished.

The second force emanates from the structure and value system of our universities, where specialty and segmentation of activity are rewarded. Curriculum becomes the province of subject matter specialists who rarely emerge from their scholarly work to collaborate with fellow specialists in considering the school curriculum as a whole. Learning is left to the psychologists, who themselves are divided in their views. The monitoring and improvement of instruction is assigned to the school supervisor.

The outcome of all this segmentation is a model of supervision known as production supervision. The school supervisor's charge is to effect the implementation and improvement of instructional practice. The "what" and "why" of the curriculum are determined from above or from external authority. Conceptualization, implementation, and evaluation are treated in isolation instead of in interdependence in defining the process of education.

The dysfunction of this artificial separation is seen in the evaluation component. Outcomes are assessed through minimum competency testing and standardized achievement testing. Teachers, under pressure to demonstrate productivity, proceed to teach to the test. The test, then, determines the curriculum and the modes of teaching.

Production supervision thrives during periods of educational retrenchment. The past back-to-basics decade has returned us to the late nineteenth century, in which the factory system required that the schools provide children with the fundamental skills of literacy and ciphering. In the name of raising standards, the educative process is reduced to the lowest common denominator of minimum competencies. Workbooks, ditto sheets, and mechanistic processes convey the message to the learner that the school is a narrow-minded workplace of drill in factual information and mechanical skills.

Facts and skills are severed from application and from significant meanings in the life of the learner. As teachers demonstrate results by teaching to the test, politicians triumphantly claim that test scores are rising without an incremental investment in the education budget.

But politicians come and go, while the schools must stay. Recent reports of the National Assessment of Educational Progress tell us that the back-to-basics retrenchment has resulted in a decline in thinking abilities and in the ability of students to make knowledge applications (NAEP, 1983).

In effective classrooms and schools, students are vitally engaged in meaningful learning activity, in cooperative planning with the teacher and fellow students, in learning responsible self-direction and social responsibility in the learning community. Under the production model of supervision, the research on effective schools has often been interpreted and applied mechanistically. This tendency is the inevitable result of seeking to reduce schooling to a narrow production perspective.

Oddly, judging from the literature in educational administration, many school administrators appear to have no objection to being cast in the role of manager along the lines of business or industry (Callahan, 1962). But the success of education cannot be measured in the same way as in business or industry.

In Mark Twain's *Gilded Age,* the entrepreneur could boast, "I wasn't worth a cent two years ago and now I owe two million dollars.''

Success in business or industry is based upon the profitable production of end products. But people are not end products. American education is concerned, not with end points, but with creating turning points in the lives of people.

The chief responsibility of school administrators is not management, but leadership. Management is concerned narrowly with doing things right; leadership is concerned broadly with doing the right things.

Clinical Supervision

In *Supervision and Education: Problems and Practices* (Tanner and Tanner, 1987), the authors trace the evolution of educational supervision and evaluate the contrasting models of supervision. Today, a considerable portion of the literature appears to be centered on what is called "clinical supervision."

The concept of clinical supervision emerged from Harvard's Master of Arts in Teaching (MAT) program in conjunction with the Newton, Mass., public schools during the late 1950s. Actually, the origins of the MAT program can be traced back to 1926, under the leadership of President Conant at Harvard, but it failed to catch on during a time of economic depression and an oversupply of teachers.

Conant, in *The Education of American Teachers* (1963), proposed that the supervision of students in the practice teaching or internship phase of their preparation be conducted under the direction of a clinical professor whose status would be "analogous to that of a clinical professor in certain medical schools.''

Conant reached the conclusion that "there are certain educational sciences bearing the same relation to the training of teachers that the medical sciences bear to the training of doctors; these sciences are not yet as well developed as their counterparts in a school of medicine, but nevertheless there is a function to be fulfilled by those who may be regarded as intermediaries between the basic social sciences and the future practitioner.''

Conant went on to describe the function of the clinical supervising professor. The clinical professor would be an outstanding teacher, abreast of all significant developments in the educational sciences, but not expected to conduct research or to publish. The clinical professor might hold a joint appointment with the college or university and a cooperating school district. Conant held that this approach would go far to raise the prestige of the classroom teacher, as well as to improve an essential but poorly supported phase of preservice teacher preparation.

It must be emphasized that the basic sciences do not determine the problems of medicine. Those problems are ascertained through the art and science of the practice of medicine. The basic sciences are utilized for their application to medical problems.

In the same way, the behavioral sciences should not determine educational problems, but only inform the professional practice of the art and science of education. At this point, it is important to remember that clinical medicine is focused mainly on the treatment of disease and illness in the controlled environment of the clinic, whereas educational supervision is conducted mainly in the naturalistic setting of the classroom and school.

In his book, *The Scientific Basis of the Art of Teaching* (1978), N.L. Gage draws an apt analogy between the practice of medicine and teaching.

"In medicine," Gage comments, "where the scientific base is unquestionable, the artistic elements also abound."

In teaching, where the artistic elements are unquestionable, a scientific base can also be developed. Unfortunately, clinical supervision as treated in the literature is segmentally focused on improving the delivery of classroom instruction, whereas the content of curriculum and other problems of schoolwide or districtwide import are relegated to higher levels of administration. Despite the fact that clinical supervision attempts to establish collegial working relations between the supervisor and teacher, the approach remains personalized-consultative and limited largely to the individual teacher in the individual classroom.

Democratic-Participatory or Developmental Supervision

Clinical supervision contrasts sharply with the holistic approach of democratic-participatory supervision. In the latter, individuals are engaged as members of a professional faculty who jointly seek solutions for educational improvement through the application of the best available evidence. In *Supervision in Education,* (Tanner and Tanner, 1987) have termed this approach developmental or professional supervision.

The teacher is regarded as a professional rather than as a technician. The supervisor is not viewed as an inspector, or a production overseer, or a counselor, or a consultant, but works collaboratively with teachers to improve all aspects of the educational program. Curriculum and teaching, the ends and the means, are seen as interdependent and continuous.

A long-standing dilemma exists in providing supervisory help to teachers without posing the threat of evaluation. In the literature of educational administration, we are told that the resolution lies in the separation of the two functions—ascribing the helping function to the supervisor as a staff consultant, and the evaluation function to the principal or other administrator as a line manager.

But this kind of division of authority and role is dysfunctional. In many of our schools, the principal is also required to perform supervisory functions. Even if there is a working division of authority and function, an unncessary dualism is created between the tasks of administration and supervision, between the pursuit of the wider mission of the school and the improvement of the education process.

The solution to this long-standing dilemma is deceptively simple. If teachers were evaluated on the basis of the openness and capability to identify problems and seek solutions, they would be less apt to devote so much energy to concealing problems. Moreover, they would be cooperatively engaged with supervisors, curriculum directors, and administrators in the evaluation of those problems and solutions. The historic antithesis between supervision and evaluation would fade away.

Under inspection and production supervision, problems are regarded as deficiencies or weaknesses. The school administrator is concerned with demonstrated success. Success can best be pursued, not by problem solving, but by following whatever kind of reform happens to be dominant at a particular time—whether it be the new math, humanizing the schools, career education, back-to-basics, behavioral objectives, or minimum competencies. If the quickest path to raising scores on a state minimum competency test or on a college entry test is by teaching to the test, then teach-to-the-test is the prevailing attitude.

Under clinical supervision, the problems addressed are limited to instructional delivery in the classroom. But educational problems have a way of extending throughout the curriculum, the faculty, the student body, the school, and into the community. In clinical supervision, the psychology is eclectic, but the process often takes the form of a kind of ego counseling for the teacher. It is largely confined to the individual teacher, and the relationship between supervisor and teacher is consultative rather than fully participative.

Moreover, clinical supervision often restricts the improvement of instruction by utilizing instruments for measuring and categorizing the overt behavior of teachers and students. These instruments tend to be mechanistic and incapable of portraying the scope and substance of the teaching-learning process.

In developmental supervision, codified knowledge and the ways of knowing are treated in vital interdependence; the unity of curriculum and instruction is recognized. The focus in developmental supervision on problem solving through reflective thinking engages the supervisor, the teacher, and students in a common mission. Full use is made of the advances in cognitive psychology in organizing the curriculum and instruction for optimum learner growth.

In developmental supervision, the entire professional staff works collaboratively on the identification and diagnosis of problems and the development of solutions for educational improvement. The entire professional staff participates conjointly in educational policy making, in curriculum development, and in the professional growth of teachers. Educational progress is made by revealing, not concealing, problems, and by marshalling the expertise of the entire professional staff.

In this way, the scientific basis of the art of supervision is revealed and advanced, and systematic formation obviates the need for educational reform. Educational "formers" replace reformers. And as Horace Mann commented, "One former is worth a thousand reformers."

References

Callahan, R.E. *Education and the Cult of Efficiency.* Chicago, Ill.: University of Chicago Press, 1962.

Caswell, H.L. *Education in the Elementary School.* New York: American Book, 1942.

Clement, J.A. "Supervision of Instruction in Secondary Schools as a Complementary Process." *Educational Administration and Supervision,* March 1927.

Conant, J.B. *The Education of American Teachers.* New York: McGraw-Hill, 1963.

Cremin, L.A. "Curriculum-Making in the United States." *Teachers College Record,* December 1971.

Dewey, J. (1899). In *Lectures in the Philosophy of Education,* edited by R.D. Archambault. New York: Random House, 1966.

Gage, N.L. *The Scientific Basis of the Art of Teaching.* New York: Teachers College Press, 1978.

Myrdal, G. *An American Dilemma.* New York: Harper, 1962.

National Assessment of Educational Progress. *NAEP Newsletter,* Winter 1983.

Tanner, D., and Tanner, L.N. *Supervision in Education: Problems and Practices.* New York: Macmillan, 1987.

Chapter 4
Productive Time and Subject Matter Learning

Herbert J. Walberg

THE NATIONAL COMMISSION for Excellence in Education, in *A Nation at Risk* (1983), and subsequent educational reform reports have called attention to two ancient adages about learning:
- Time matters; practice makes perfect.
- Content or subject matter also matters; students learn what they do while learning.

Many recent educational reforms, particularly those proposed and enacted by governors and legislators, have emphasized these two truisms; and psychological research confirms the likelihood of their efficacy and wisdom. Time and content offer convenient ways to measure the curriculum; they do not capture all that is important about what the curriculum offers, but they can serve as critical dimensions for planning and evaluating curriculum offerings.

The purpose of this chapter is to review recent research on learning in relation to time and subject matter content, and to raise some of the implications for curricular analysis.

Educators must recognize how precious time is, if for no other reason than it is such a scarce resource. In the life of typical students, "allocated time" in school during the first 18 years of life constitutes only about 8 percent of all hours (and 13 percent of the waking hours). Absences, lateness, inattention, disruptions, and unsuitable instruction take up some of this allocated time.

"Engaged time," or "time on task" may be considerably less than the 8 percent of time nominally allocated for schooling. The quality as well as the quantity of time are important determinants of how much is learned; therefore, stimulating and rigorous instruction that leads to "learning time" or "productive time" is also needed.

Allocated time has steadily expanded during this century. The average number of years of education in the U.S. adult population, for example, has steadily increased (Finn, 1987).

Educators, parents, and policymakers have also recently begun a variety of programs to increase learning time in other ways. These include preschool, half-day and full-day kindergarten, active parental work with youngsters at home, and encouraging them to watch and analyze constructive television programs.

Instructional methods and motivational techniques have been introduced to increase engaged time in schools: more homework with feedback, extended-day school with academic encouragement and assistance, and summer school for children who fall behind. Some districts and states are increasing the number of days in the regular school year and the number of hours in the school day. Some are mandating content, often by requiring courses in core subjects such as English, mathematics, science, civics, history, geography, and foreign languages (Doyle and Hartle, 1985; Finn, 1987). Some are attempting to work with dropouts to keep more students in school for a longer time.

Psychological Perspectives on Educational Time

Since Socrates, psychological views of the learner have influenced educational theory and practice. Current psychological research provides some useful insights on time and learning. This section discusses recent discoveries in cognitive psychology and theories of instruction and explores whether time-consuming and difficult work causes psychological harm.

Insights from Cognitive Psychology

Psychological phenomena can often best be understood by the study of extreme cases. Creativity and talent are cases in point. Until recently, these traits have been intuitively thought of as innate or accidental. But contrary to the notion of instant creativity that was popular in the 1960s, great accomplishments are the result of opportunity and of continuous, concentrated effort for at least a decade. For example, when Isaac Newton was asked how he had managed to surpass the discoveries of his predecessors, he replied, "By always thinking about them." The eminent mathematician Friedrich Gauss said, "If others would but reflect on mathematical truths as deeply and continuously as I have, they would make my discoveries."

So, too, are accomplishments in many other areas. Psychological studies of the lives of eminent painters, writers, musicians, philosophers, religious leaders, and scientists of previous centuries, as well as those of prize winning adolescents in this country today, reveal early, intense concentration on previous work in their fields, often to the near exclusion of other activities. It appears that science and mathematics, because of their highly specialized and abstract symbolism, may require even greater concentration and perseverance (Csikszentmihalyi, 1982; Walberg, in press).

The same fundamental thought processes appear to be required in both elementary and advanced study (Simon, 1981). The acquisition of information and problem solving by beginners differ in degree rather than in kind from the mental activities of experts. The scarce resources are time and concentration rather than the available information or the processing capacity of the mind. Both of these, for practical purposes, seem unlimited.

Simon's work shows that, aside from motivation and opportunity, the constraints on the acquisition of knowledge are the few items of information, perhaps two to seven, that humans can hold in conscious memory, and the time required—5 to 10 seconds—to store an item in long-term memory. Experts differ from novices in science, chess, and other fields not only in having more information in permanent memory but also, and more significantly, in being able to process it efficiently.

Among experts, for example, items of information are more thoroughly indexed and can be rapidly brought to conscious memory. The items are elaborately associated or linked with one another. Two consequences of these associations are the ability to recover information by alternative links even when parts of the direct indexing are lost, and the capacity for trial-and-error searches. These essential routines are called into play in problem solving from the most elementary to the most advanced levels.

The greatest advantage of the expert, and, conversely, the biggest problem for the novice attempting to learn cognitively demanding material, is "chunking"—the representation of abstract groups of items as linked clusters that can be efficiently processed as an ensemble. Chunks may underlie mental processes ranging from the childhood stages of cognitive development identified by Jean Piaget, to scientific discoveries.

Simon (1981) estimates that about 50 thousand chunks, the same magnitude as the recognition vocabulary of college-educated readers, may be required for the expert mastery of a special field. The highest achievements in various disciplines, however, may require a memory store of one million chunks. This level of expertise may take even the talented about a decade of 70 hours per week of concentrated effort to acquire, although seven to nine-year-old exceptions such as Mozart and Bobbie Fisher can be cited.

The prospect of such prodigious and sustained concentration may impress, if not daunt, even the talented. Yet, only a small fraction of that total is required for impressive achievement. Only an extra hour or two per day may enable beginners to attain results far beyond unpracticed adults in many fields.

Youth of normal intelligence possess the requisite talent for respectable attainments; they can acquire the information and skills that constitute a small but important part of what experts command. The data on achievement test scores of youngsters in the United States and other countries (discussed in a subsequent section) suggest that this fraction can be raised considerably.

Hard Work: An Unlikely Culprit

Some educators fear that American youngsters cannot sustain the long hours necessary to achieve well by international standards. They apparently believe that either heredity or American culture prevents students from learning, and that to press them further might result in psychological stress, unhappiness, heart disease, suicide, and the like.

Although such fears are frequently expressed, little research supports them. Indeed, some evidence suggests that effortful, constructive engagement enhances psychological well-being.

One source of anxiety about difficult academic work stems from analogies drawn from speculation that a "Type A behavior pattern, manifested primarily by competitiveness, excessive drive, and enhanced sense of time urgency" causes coronary heart disease (Shekelle, 1985).

The largest surveys, however, show that this pattern does not predict greater incidence of coronary disease (Shekelle, 1985).

Moreover, a synthesis of 83 studies of psychological predictors of heart disease concluded: "The picture of coronary-proneness revealed by this review is not one of a hurried, impatient workaholic but instead is one of a person with one or more negative emotions," such as hostility and depression (Booth-Kewley and Friedman, 1987, p. 343).

What about suicides of hard-working Japanese students, well-known for their prodigious amounts of study? For ages 10 to 19, Japanese suicide rates per 100 thousand in 1984 were about half the U.S. rates, which had more than doubled since 1963. This was a period, according to U.S. education reform reports, of slackened educational standards and declining student effort.

Does effort cause unhappiness? Psychological research on optimal and exhilarating experiences shows that life's greatest pleasures include the development of skills, and absorption in constructive activities (Czikszentmihalyi, 1982; Argyle, 1987).

Research on adults, moreover, shows that such experiences are more often encountered in work than in leisure. High school students encounter them when opportunities sufficiently challenge their skills both in school and in outside pursuits (Csikszentmihalyi, 1982).

To be sure, students can work too hard. But average students seem far from that danger if for no other reason than that they watch nearly as much television as they spend in school during the academic year (Walberg and Shanahan, 1983). Television is sedentary. It is passive. It displaces homework, leisure reading, and active pursuits.

Although time and effort hardly seem to cause undue stress, too much external pressure, of course, can produce anxiety. If students feel driven by parents and teachers, if they fall far behind their peers and have little hope of catching up, if they blame themselves for failure to attain perfection, if they lose a sense of control and autonomy, then they can become depressed and feel helpless (Abramson, Seligman, and Teasdale, 1978). Encouragement, the setting of realistic goals, support and recognition for accomplishment, and learning for its own sake are preferred incentives over external pressure.

Amount and Quality of Time

In recent years, several breakthroughs have occurred in the analyses of large-scale educational surveys and in the syntheses of thousands of educational research results. (See Walberg, 1984b, 1986, for details.) These surveys and syntheses show that nine factors increase learning. Potent, consistent, and widely generalizable, these nine factors fall into the three groups show in Table I.

Collectively, the various studies suggest that these nine factors are powerful and consistent in influencing learning. Syntheses of about 2,575 studies suggest that these generalizable factors are the chief influences on academic achievement and, more broadly, on school-related cognitive, affective, and behavioral learning. Many aspects of the factors, especially the amount and quality of instruction, can be altered by educators. The factors deserve our attention, especially in improving educational opportunities for at-risk youth.

Each of the first five factors—prior achievement, development, motivation, and the quantity and quality of instruction—seems necessary for learning in school. Without at least a small amount of each, the student can learn little. Large amounts of instruction and high degrees of ability, for example, may count for little if students are unmotivated or instruction is unsuitable.

If these findings are combined with insights from cognitive psychology (discussed above), it is easy to see why time is a central and irreducible ingredient among the alterable factors in learning. First, recall that the acquisition of an item of information requires an estimated 5 to 10 seconds; relating it "meaningfully" to assimilated chunks requires additional seconds; and problem solving or discovery by the trial-and-error combining of chunks may take minutes, hours, days, or years.

But not all time allocated for school and outside study is directed to these fundamental processes of learning and discovery. Quality of instruction, for example, can be understood as providing optimal cues, correctives, and reinforcement to ensure the fruitfulness of engaged time.

Diagnosis and tutoring can help ensure that instruction is suitable to the individual student. Inspired teaching can enhance motivation to keep students persevering. Quality of instruction, then, may be thought of as efficient enhancement of allocated or engaged learning time.

Similarly, the four psychological environments in the productivity model can enlarge and enhance learning time. Good classroom morale may reflect match of the lesson to student aptitude, the socially-stimulating characteristics of the academic group, or in general, the degree to which students are concentrating on learning rather than on unconstructive outcomes. Peer groups outside school and stimulating home environments also can help by enlarging learning time and enhancing its efficiency.

Table 1

Nine Educational Productivity Factors

Student Aptitude
1. *Ability or* preferably *prior achievement* as measured by the usual achievement tests.
2. *Development* as indexed by chronological age or stage of maturation.
3. *Motivation or self-concept* as indicated by personality tests or the student's willingness to persevere intensively on learning tasks.

Instruction
4. The *amount of time* students engage in learning.
5. The *quality of the instructional experience* including method (psychological) and curricular (content) aspects.

Psychological Environments
6. The *"curriculum of the home."*
7. The *morale of classroom* social group.
8. The *peer group outside school.*
9. *Minimum* leisure-time *television* viewing.

Finally, television can displace homework, leisure reading, and other stimulating activities. It may dull the student's keenness for academic work. Some of the average of 28 hours a week high school students say they spend viewing television might usefully be added to the mere 4 or 5 weekly hours of homework they report (Walberg and Shanahan, 1983).

Matthew Effects

Students who are behind at the beginning of schooling or who are slow to start often learn at a slower rate. Those who start ahead gain at a faster rate, resulting in what has been called "Matthew effects".[1] (See Walberg and Tsai, 1983.)

This notion characterizes school learning, family influences on development, and socioeconomic advantages in communication among adults (Walberg and Tsai, 1983), as well as the development of reading comprehension and verbal literacy (Stanovitch, 1986). Ironically, although improved instructional programs may benefit all students, they may confer greater advantages on those who are initially advantaged. For this reason, the first six years of life and the "curriculum of the home" are decisive influences on academic achievement (Walberg, 1984a; U.S. Department of Education, 1986).

Stevenson, Lee, and Stigler (1986) provide a striking illustration of the Matthew effects. These authors carefully observed and tested Japanese, Taiwanese, and American students in elementary school mathematics classes. Cross-nationally calibrated I.Q. tests showed that all three groups were equally able at the start of schooling, but with each year, Asian students drew further ahead in achievement. A small achievement advantage at the end of the first grade grew ever larger, so that by fifth grade, the worst Asian class in the sample exceeded the best American class.

The Asian students had a far more rigorous curriculum and worked at a faster pace. They studied far more at school and, with their parents' encouragement, at home, especially those who temporarily fell behind in achievement.

In the United States, success was more often attributed to ability; in Asia, to hard work. Like racial, ethnic, and special-education classifications, ability tests may encourage a belief in educational predestination rather than in effort, the amount and quality of instruction, and parental involvement as keys to achievement.

Time in School

Kemmerer's (1978-79) compilation of statistical indexes of the amount of time spent in school shows impressive gains for the period 1890-1974. The median number of school years completed by the adult population rose from 8.2 to 12.3. But Japan currently graduates about 96 percent of its students from high school, in contrast to 75 percent in the United States. Japanese schools have 240 days per year in contrast to 180 in the United States. And Japanese students engage in far more extramural study (National Commission on Excellence in Education, 1983; U.S. Department of Education, 1987).

Kemmerer's compilations show that time allocated for specific subject matter varies widely across communities: Ratios of highest to lowest time

---

[1] From Matthew, XXV, 29: "For unto every one that hath shall be given, and he shall have abundance; but from him that hath not shall be taken away even that which he hath."

allocations varied 144 to 1 and 109 to 1 in science and literature, 12 to 1 and 4 to 1 in reading and mathematics. Within one district, students' exposure to schooling varied from 710 to 1,150 hours per year. Kemmerer also noted that absence rates are often higher in urban than suburban schools.

Berliner (1979) and Rosenshine (1980) reported wide variations in classroom time allocations and engaged time. More recently. Dreeben and Barr (1987) noted similar wide variations in time allocated to reading and in the amount of subject matter covered. Coverage was positively related to the amount of time allocated, difficulty of the material, and average student aptitude in the group. (A subsequent section of this review deals with the generally positive effect of content coverage on learning.)

How much time is needed to learn? This question cannot be answered in absolute terms because it depends on what is to be learned, how it is taught, and the student's aptitude. Gettinger (1987) has provided some interesting estimates of time required by fastest and slowest learners in various settings.

For a seven-month period, for example, the number of problems completed in computer-assisted instruction varied from about 1,000 to 5,000. Programmed-instruction research showed that students took from 1 to 60 days to complete a unit. When ratios of elapsed time by fastest and slowest learners to reach criterion performance in ordinary classrooms are calculated (Frederick and Walberg, 1980), variations run from 1.7 to 7.1 (Gettinger, 1987).

Productive Time: A New Conception

Substantial variations in time needed to learn suggest that the same instructional content and pace will not be optimal for typical classes of students, since some students may already know what is taught, and others may be incapable of learning it until they master prerequisite skills. A number of programs such as mastery learning, cooperative learning, acceleration, tutoring, computer-assisted instruction, adaptive instruction, and diagnostic-prescriptive instruction have a good record of accommodating individual differences (Walberg, 1984b).

Because of Matthew effects, such programs are appropriate both in elementary schools to prevent slower students from falling far behind, and in high schools to afford these students more time and remedial instruction to catch up with their peers.

The evolving psychological theory of individual differences suggests a new insight with educational implications for instructional improvement efforts. First, recall that only about 8 percent of a student's time is spent in school. Second, scholars such as Berliner (1979) and Rosenshine (1980) showed that only a fraction of allocated time is engaged time or time on task when students are studying or attending to lessons.

More rare and precious still is academic learning time, or productive time, when students are actually learning, either from lessons or individual differences and by teaching study skills so that students themselves can concentrate more fully on what is required.

All other things being equal, increases in allocated and engaged time are effective, but expanding productive time is both effective and efficient since it increases student learning while conserving available time.

Content Is Consequential

Educators cannot raise achievement by simply mandating courses. Teachers and students may lack the ability and motivation for foreign languages, physics, higher mathematics, and other demanding courses. By themselves, such mandates may mean higher dropout rates. (Low standards, however, debase high school diplomas). Higher standards and rigorous courses are likely to work best when the amount of time, homework, the quality of instruction, classroom morale, and parental involvement are simultaneously enhanced or expanded.

The amount of time spent on learning can be indexed (albeit imprecisely) by how many courses students take in a given subject and the number of items of content their teachers cover during a course or year. Studies in the United States and other countries show that such indexes are strongly associated with how much students learn.

The International Association for the Evaluation of Educational Achievement (IEA) first showed compellingly the powerful effects of content exposure on learning. Although such exposure may not vary much within countries, especially those with strong central ministries of education such as France and Japan, it varies widely among countries. The IEA group measured content exposure in various ways, including the number of courses, hours of time spent on content during the subject year, standards, and test items covered in classes.

These exposure indexes were among the most strong and consistent correlates of learning within and across countries. Even controlled for other productivity factors, these indexes typically yielded significant weights in multiple regression analyses. They were demonstrated in civics, English, French, other languages, literature, mathematics, reading comprehension, and science (Postlethwaite, 1975, 28-29; Walberg, Harnisch, and Tsai, 1986).

In the United States, the National Assessment of Educational Progress (NAEP) offers further evidence of the powerful effects of content exposure. The effects can be seen in analyses of data at several age levels in reading, social studies, and science (Walberg, 1986), but emerge most clearly in high school mathematics because of the general consensus about the subject matter.

On the NAEP mathematics test for 17-year-olds, for example, the test scores correlated .63 with the rated vigor of the highest course taken (ranging from consumer mathematics to calculus), and .62 with the number of mathematics courses completed. These correlations probably come close to the upper limit that surveys of content measures can provide within the ordinary range of variation.

Curriculum Alignment

To the extent that the curriculum can be measured in time and content, educational goals, curriculum materials and activities, tests, and other assessment tools can be coordinated with one another (cf. Chapter 1). Materials and activities can follow from goals, and evaluation can assess the degree to which the means attain the goals. Districts, departments, and individual teachers contribute to curricular efficiency by explicit specification, coordination, and evaluation of their chief ends and means—student learning outcomes and instructional resources.

Conclusion

Time is one of nine determinants of academic learning. Most studies of allocated and engaged time show consistent but modest effects. By several indexes, the amount of time devoted to schooling in the United States has increased substantially during the twentieth century. But it is difficult to argue that the time allocated is yet sufficient, given the increasing cognitive demands of the job market, poor achievement scores of U.S. students by international standards, and the some 28 hours that typical students spend watching television each week.

Raising time allocations and engaging students for a greater fraction of allocated time are likely to help learning. Requiring typical students to study longer hardly seems a threat to their well-being. But increasing productive time—that fraction of class and individual study time when students actually learn—is even more important. Ordinarily, only a fraction of engaged time is productive.

Conventional whole-group instruction cannot accommodate the vast differences in student learning rates and prior knowledge, nor the needs of students with weak study skills who study without learning.

To accommodate these differences and reduce Matthew effects, instruction can be made more suitable to individual learners, and students can be taught to concentrate more fully on what they individually need to know. Productive time is both effective and efficient, since it increases human achievement and conserves valuable time. Indeed, matching educational opportunities to individual skills appears to be rewarding and fulfilling in itself.

References

Abramson, L.Y.; Seligman, M.E.P.; and Teasdale, J.D. "Learned Helplessness in Humans." *Journal of Abnormal Psychology* 87 (1978):49-74.

Argyle, M. *The Psychology of Happiness*. London: Mehuen, 1987.

Berliner, D.C. "Tempus Educare." In *Research on Teaching,* edited by P.L. Peterson and H.J. Walberg. Berkeley, Calif.: McCutchan Publishing, 1979.

Booth-Kewley, S., and Friedman, H.S. "Psychological Predictors of Heart Disease: A Quantitative Review." *Psychological Bulletin* 101 (1987):343-62.

Csikszentmihalyi, M. "Toward a Psychology of Optimal Experience." *Review of Personality and Social Psychology* 45 (1982):317-18.

Doyle, D.P., and Hartle, T.W. *Excellence in Education: The States Take Charge*. Washington, D.C.: American Enterprise Institute, 1985.

Dreeben, R., and Barr, R. "An Organizational Analysis of Curriculum and Instruction." In *The Social Organization of Schools,* edited by M.T. Hallinan. New York: Plenun Press, 1987.

Finn, Jr., C.E. "The High School Dropout Puzzle." *The Public Interest,* Spring 1987.

Frederick, W.C., and Walberg, H.J. "Learning as a Function of Time." *Journal of Educational Research* 73 (1980):183-94.

Gettinger, M. "Individual Differences in Time Needed for Learning. A Review of Literature." *Educational Psychologist* 19 (1987): 15-29.

Kemmerer, F. "The Allocation of Student Time." *Administrator's Notebook* 27 (1978-79):1-4.

National Commission on Excellence in Education. *A Nation at Risk: The Imperative for School Reform*. Washington, D.C.: U.S. Government Printing Office, 1983.

Postlethwaite, T.N. *School Organization and Student Achievement*. Stockholm, Sweden: Almqvist and Wissell, 1975.

Rosenshine, B. "How Time Is Spent in Elementary School Classrooms." In *Time to Learn,* edited by C. Denham and Ann Lieberman. Washington, D.C.: U.S. Department of Education, 1980.

Shekelle, R.B. "The MRFIT Behavior Pattern Study." *American Journal of Epidemiology* 122 (1985):559-70.

Simon, H.A. *Sciences of the Artificial*. Cambridge, Mass.: MIT Press, 1981.

Stanovitch, K.E. "Matthew Effects in Reading: Some Consequences of Individual Differences in the Acquisitions of Literacy." *Reading Research Quarterly* 21 (1986):360-407.

Stevenson, H.W.; Lee, S.Y.; and Stigler, J.W. "Mathematics Achievement of Chinese, Japanese, and American Children." *Science* 231 (1986):693-99.

U.S. Department of Education. *What Works: Research About Teaching and Learning*. Washington, D.C.: DOE, 1986.

Walberg, H.J. "Families as Partners in Educational Productivity." *Phi Delta Kappan* 84 (1984a):397-400.

———. "Improving the Productivity of America's Schools." *Edcational Leadership* 41 (1984b):19-27.

———. "Synthesis of Research on Teaching." In *Handbook of Research on Teaching*, edited by M.C. Wittrock. New York: Macmillan, 1986.

———. "Talent as Learning." In *The Nature of Creativity,* edited by R.L. Sternberg. New York: Oxford University Press, in press.

Walberg, H.J., and Shanahan, T. "High School Effects on Individual Students." *Educational Researcher* 12 (1983):4-9.

Walberg, H.J., and Tsai, S.-L. "Matthew Effects in Education." *American Educational Research Journal* 20 (1983):359-73.

Walberg, H.J.; Harnisch, D.; Tsai, S.-L. "School Productivity in Twelve Countries." *British Journal of Educational Research* 12 (1986):237-48.